Gnome Balcony

Ross Kightly

Happen*Stance*

Acknowledgements:
Thanks are due to editors of the following magazines where some of these
poems were first published: *Envoi, Pennine Platform, The Rialto.*

Note:

In 'A Soft Answer' (page 32), the Italian sentence *No, ma per voi, gentilissimi Signori, imparerei volentieri* translates into English as 'No, but for you, most kind gentlemen, I'd gladly learn.'

Printed by The Dolphin Press
www.dolphinpress.co.uk

Published in 2011 by Happen*Stance*
21 Hatton Green, Glenrothes, Fife KY7 4SD
nell@happenstancepress.com
www.happenstancepress.com

Orders:
Individual pamphlets £4.00 (includes UK p&p).
Please make cheques payable to Happen*Stance* or order
through PayPal in the website shop.

CONTENTS

for
Chris

Bergamo

we don't have to go   we can sit here
        and the sun will move behind us slowly
                people on the plain go home
        allowing us to do our disappearing trick

be very careful with that sharp little knife
        some cheese   half a panino   tomato   salami
                a light luncheon   no burden to bring it here
        just the single bottle of cool wine

Llangrannog

The faint feathery comet is a disappointment.
Tide on the make in the moonlight,
the railing cold as I move my hand along.
I find your hand waiting.

A sound. In the house? Under the dark headland?
Is your life rearranging furniture,
making a space for me to move in?
If so, the comet must be judged a disappointment.

To tell the truth

Even back then, I knew it couldn't last.
You told me so yourself with the surf's roar
in our ears that night on the beach. My thirst
was still, of course, unsatisfied. From where
you'd let my hand reach, there was some response
though soon repressed—perhaps no more than fright.
You were 'good' and not 'like that', so your sense
sent us back to our separate tents. Night,

you told me several times, is no place for
deciding important things, and so we
made all decisions in bright light, clear, far
from dark and sinister emotions. See
how I have honoured this pact. I never
look at those photos at night, not ever.

Irritants

STRENGTH
is the longest one-syllable word in English.

I find this out somehow using the clue 'Power'.

In every puzzle is a resolution:
WHITE ELEPHANT—'an unwanted possession'—
something I have but no longer desire,
clues to the things learned in the dark,
where all the deeds, real or imaginary,
are stored.

And this is like knowing if I'm pulled over,
it won't just be breathalysing
but opening the boot where the body is bundled in carpet

though if I roll over, tuck the numb arm comfortably,
think of you, it will all go away.
                                        The power
to make things as they ought to be is given
freely. OPULENT is wealthy.

How many midges breed each year in Scotland?
Somebody must have CALCULATED
(worked out) a total: it's the sort of thing they do.

If I wake and make myself comfortable
and reach out to find you breathing deeply
next to (BESIDE) me, the stings are million
but pathetically painless.

Gnome balcony

I miss Tyehra. Our romance
may have been brief, passing as swiftly as
the stroke of his brush across her hair,
her cerulean eye, her so perfectly restrained swell
of bodice, but we were made for each other.

In the Case, we stood side by side, my elbow
just touching her marshmallow-plump shoulder,
her exquisitely delineated smile turned towards
my roguish, still virile grin of mischievous
anticipation, her basket for the mushrooms ever
tapping gently against the butt of my rifle.
No fishing-rod for me! I've always been
a hunting gnome.

So here I am, crammed in, high above the blessed earth,
miles from the forest, from the blissful aroma
of tree-trunks going back to soil. I'm crushed
amongst these crude travesties, these epitomes of debasement,
these mass-produced, garden-centre clones.

Oh the old chap and his missus are
kind enough. They keep the pot-plants watered here.
The lurid foliage obscures the 'view'. But
there is no-one here of Tyehra's sweet intelligence.
Where is she now? Is she somehow in our natural
element, the loam, gathering mushrooms
in some garden, thinking of—not me, of course.

Yesterday I felt the first tickling, insidious hint
of algae in my elbow's crook, the one that cradles
my useless rifle.

Boy with a hatchet

I only wanted respect. Not too much to ask,
you'd think, with all the sweat and tears I put in—
but no, it was always, 'Jack do *this*! Jack do
that! Jack do every bloody thing!' And the
beatings . . . I could show you the scars
and weals, but I've got too much pride . . . at my age
you wouldn't expect a lot of 'business sense'—
and the way *she* made it sound, the Old Lady,
you'd think those beans were really made of
solid gold—and our old cow. . . . Well, let me tell
you, another week and she'd have been glue
and candles. No good trying to tell me it's all
worked out fine in the end. It *was* like that,
for a little while, after the Crash—but when
the dust settled, folk stopped calling me 'Brave
Jack' and the old envy thing set in. 'What's
he ever done to deserve *that*?' you'd hear
muttered everywhere—latest thing, this—what
d'you call it? —*Editorial*—in some bloody rag.
EMBLEM OF RAMPANT OPPORTUNISM—
that's me. I copied out a bit. Cop this—'The ancient
giant of working class dignity is brought down by
a pint-sized robber baron of the new wave of
entrepreneurialism.' I ask you—
is that how you treat a kid who just
saw a few things lying around up there and
brought 'em home? Fair's fair, I say.
I don't remember there being too much
Sympathy for the Giant in the bad old days
before I got the little hatchet on the job!

ＲＯＳＳ ＫＩＧＨＴＬＹ

Haze

A decent little cooking whisky—
that's what he always says—
the thing to cut through the pesky
nonsense of Reality Haze.

My worry is he could be ruining
his palate with that supermarket
stuff. Now Islay is the real thing,
the only super-reliable skyrocket

cutting through the mush of *now*
and taking off for sometime *when*—
getting back in tune with how
you felt in the Real World back then

when all was an iodine prologue
to the clarity of Laphroig.

Winnow

every now and then
a big door would

open on the left
and the morning sun

would slant in
and laughing children

would be dancing
back-lit but colourful

rosy-cheeked dressed
in clean hand-me-downs

and a door on the right
would open

and the breeze would
slant through

whirling up with husks
and the children's laughter

Between

And then you'll turn slightly or
raise your chin at a familiar angle,
a wry twist to your lip or that
flop of your fringe over your
forehead, or you'll use a phrase
I've not heard for years and I know

how much you are other. Not me, not her,
not—really—any body but your own . . . and then
you'll be my educator, pointing out
one or two places where I got it wrong

and I'm once more at the kitchen table
more than half a century ago, and I know
I need to listen very carefully before
it's far too late to learn the skills
of being who I need to be.

Catching glimpses

the time in the Brown Cow when
the vegetarian option was off
and I hadn't properly worked out
how to see her properly

or the time in the Barum Top
and the unexpected text
and a tall blonde woman
strolling over unexpectedly

or it might be after that long journey
in Pizza Express on the Strand
and she had such a long way back
that after some talk we parted early

ROSS KIGHTLY

Graduation

I know this business isn't
what you really want to be doing just this moment.
Maybe you'd never be wanting
to pick up a degree you're not quite
completely happy with.

I know it might be awkward
considering who'll be here and having to meet up—
your mum and me—but I'm not worried—

what happened wasn't my fault—
not all of it.

And the rest of the stuff
you've had to cope with since then
and done a good job on,
even if you don't think so,
that wasn't my fault either—
not all of it.

And then later when I tell you
I'm proud of you, and you look at me ruefully
and tell me you're not likely to do anything more
that'll make me proud of you,

that's my decision.

All of it.

Even more

Buses roar across the end of the covered arcade—
we're trying to be somewhere that's not
just like it is in the town outside—
a place here with café tables
and sophisticated jazz on a discreet PA
struggling to assert itself.

I nurse a Peroni that doesn't taste quite
right, even in the sunshine, whose resonance
is amplified by the white-girdered roof.
We've even got an Eccentric, clapping
out of time and shouting the sort of song
he fancies, wrongly, fits the ambience.

But then there's a tall, broad-shouldered lad
I'd like, perhaps, to have been some time ago
in some other, even more fortunate
successful life. My smiling Doppelgänger.
Yeah—you wish! 'Sit down, son—well done
for those *results*. Do you want a Peroni. . . ?'

'Nah, San Mig's more me, old man.
Busca tres barcos, eh?'

                    That'll do.
We're both somewhere else, *and* here
and that's plenty good enough for me.

Template for understanding a city

This can be opened and laid down.
When you contemplate your city
and young women busy with chairs,
rearranging tables in quiet taverns,
do you know what they are thinking?

When you imagine your city's
hills, rising behind, where red
tractors slowly draw clouds of gulls
down undemanding slopes, do you
wake to a hint of diesel in your room?

When you see the city rolled out
in light, viewed from the lookout post,
where tail lights draw red scars
along the wide night streets,
do you feel their hot blades?

When the salt and sand fill your mouth
and the city's image folds away,
when the tongues of blood lick across
the parks and gardens, do the swords
and machetes make sense to you?

Last toast

Please allow me to raise a glass to
all you people I never really realised
were so deep inside me—all you legions
of Slags and Tarts, Hoors and Town
Bikes, you Poofs and Shirt-Lifters,
Fudge-Packers, Nancy Boys and
Queers. All you Kippers, Poms and Paddies,
Dagoes, Gyppos, Wogs and Nig-Nogs,
Malts and Balts, Slavs and Eye-ties, Greasy
Greeks and Abos, Boongs and Niggers,
Fuzzy-Wuzzy Angels. . . . Do allow me to
raise this last glass now I've realised I am
one of you, looking, sounding and therefore
being as I am a brash and brazen, loud,
opinionated, redneck MCP Aussie Larrikin
abroad—so all *we* need to do is get the
message out to the Pollies—*you know*, the
Boss Lot up in Whitehall, the ones that think
they run the show—and out to all the Seppos—
you know the Septic Tanks, the Yanks—
get it out to them, the simple message of this
Last Toast. The War on Terror's being fought
on all the wrong fields, Messrs Pres and Prime M,
Sirs. You need to point those Smart Missiles
inwards—target me and my newfound mates,
the ones who live inside your cerebellum, all
the other different and strange Outsiders, just like you—

Ross Kightly

the NineElevenGuantanamoBayAfghanistan-
IraqIranPakkieAlQuaidaNexusofEvilRagHeadTerror-
Wielding Mujahadin, Taliban, Fifth Column in
your cortex. Locked on target? Good. Fire!
At last. *On* target. Time for this final toast?

Unexpected

Ran into Mum the other day.
Not what I'd expected—her being
so far away—and *dead* of course—
but as one gets on in life oneself
one stops being so *surprised* by
things. So I pulled myself together,
smiled and started to chat—but she
was 'on a short leash,' she said,
'no questions.' I was about to ask
'Wh. . . ?' but that *look* of hers
shut me up. She told me there was
'a strict embargo' on 'certain areas' of
'confidential information'. Just one
question in the wrong place and
boff! she's gone . . . and the waiting
list's a complete *bugger!* Sorry, but
there's no other way to put it—utter
nonsense, the red tape and all. . . .
What she needed to tell me was
the Scatterings had been successful—
ashes in two bays, two continents, half
a world apart—nice *perspective*, that.
She'd chosen me, not Brother P, because . . .

she wouldn't—couldn't?—say, just
the one message she had for me—stop
worrying, stop trying to be right all the time . . .
There was this Pommie bloke she'd met—

not her type—bit *snide*, bit of a *whinger*—
used to work in libraries. Must've
liked books—just like me, she thought—
he talked a *lot* of *rot*, he did . . . one thing
made sense . . . but the LANGUAGE!
She wouldn't repeat the exact words, just
the *sense*, that somehow she and Dad were
to blame for me being like I am—then *she*
was gone . . . again . . . just the empty sky
filling up with clouds and me resolving to
do better next time—because falling short
is still what really worries the shit out of me. . . .

Landscapes

Some people on certain days will tackle
wind dust rock sand Gila Monster deserts

short blue-green freezing afternoons
on the pack-ice wrestling polar bears

even slime-green dank dark crab-scuttling
coastal caverns close to high tide

in search of skull-guarded
pirate treasure-chests

they'll balance across razor-edged ridges of
mountain ranges barefoot in shorts and t-shirt

and on some (few) future days
I might go too if you would come

but I think today tomorrow and
the next day and the day after that

I'd prefer to take the walk past the nice houses
at the Square and the swallow barn

through the gate not over it this time
and up the rocky slope laughing

past the gorse lair of the Woolly Wolf
to the wind-torn lone hawthorn

with or without the sudden curlew
that might or might not flash across

to the easy sheep slope down to
the coast the mere and the castle.

We know we can do this any day
and it will never ever fail us.

not again never

at the gate   that's where you got to wait
you can't come in   until they've checked
some datebase   I suppose
they never issued a   pass or anything
like that   too damn easy
and they're fat   fat as stuffed spring rolls

      first time there   I was naughty
I know I was   nobody said
      but I was naughty   kept touching things
I didn't ought to touch   nice things they were
      but that's no excuse   I know that
I knew then   but I kept on touching

the place is all right   at least I suppose
it's not as bad as   that dark room
the small one   I didn't like it there
with the smell of dead skin   and the fingernails
underfoot   it's not as bad as that here now
even the gate   it's painted blue

air is all right too   I suppose
      you have to breathe   even in the dark room
you had to pull it into your lungs   nasty air there
      pull it in   right down deep inside
makes me sick   just remembering
      the thick air   in the dark room

it seems all right   at the gate now
I don't mind waiting   not if I know I can get in
I like to get inside   I don't touch things I oughtn't to
not any more   I want to sometimes
the soft things   I know I want to touch them
but they   don't want me to touch

    thin they said   needed not to be
I needed to swell   but I did that once—swole
    all up   it hurt
that was before   the thick air in the small
    dark room   the nasty air and nails
don't want to do that   not again never

Prose of comings back

The crux of the matter the nub of the thing is
nobody who's done it ever
comes back repentant they just
can't admit it was a shit of decision
to bugger off, leave the wife and kids
all for a life that turned out
against the odds to be both more
boring and uncomfortable—
a floor is just a set of boards even if it's
in a garret in Montmartre.

I want to hear it for the three esses—
for a comfy hygienic shit on
sterile porcelain (and not over
a long drop in the short back yard
of a flop-house in Cairns), a
shave with a proper Wilkinson Sword or Gillette or
even a Philishave. I don't condone
product placement but . . .
and a shampoo, preferably medicated—and not
a blow dry but a gentle sun bake
in a quiet suburban backyard in Cheam or Penge,
Moorabbin, Springvale, or even—God help us—
in Todmorden!

Rats

They share your goods regardless.
They live in the dark. They come out and take
what suits them.
                          Schoolkids swapped stories:
screaming children suddenly stilled;
fathers' earlobes missing in the night;
rats snuggled in bellies like backward babies.

The rat-trap's pressed-steel base
was purposeful as a bulkhead.
'Keep your bloody fingers clear—' said Dad.
'—this'd chop them off like celery!'
The trap's spring groaned.

Traps. Yes, and poison. All the neighbours used them.
But who could say he'd sat up
in the sleepout window while his dad
shot at the chookhouse rats with a .303?
(I swear the big rat was hunched and fleeced,
a merino bison.)

Searching the workshop loft three decades later
I found a papery, alopoeciac mummy,
faded grey and light as cobwebs.
I couldn't bring myself to ease at last
the spring and lift the burden
from the grinning broken neck.
Under a paper-lip, the front teeth still
were neat and sharp.

Course work

The Mole glides by its rolling bank
and manor house and church are still.
With voices bright and laughter frank
two strolling learners chat their fill.

A hoar frost decorates the grass
and crunches as the strolling two,
transformed by moonlight, slowly pass
beyond a tidy hedge of yew

to where, below the tinselled weir
the river threatens choking death
and little gasps of pleasant fear
enlarge her clouds of foggy breath.

She whispers: 'Would you rescue me
if I slipped in?' He's nearly cowed
but knows he can't ignore the plea
and knows too what's not yet avowed

and so he says, 'Don't slip, take care,
hold tight—I'm steady as a rock!'
Then hand-in-hand this new-made pair
walk silent past the church tower clock.

I chose this house because

it has small windows with blue and white shutters
there are two pints of red-top and one of silver-top daily
they have fireworks in November and snow at Christmas
crocuses and daffodils bloom in spring and roses in summer
a dog and a cat live there and happily play together
the children squabble gently when they wave goodbye
they leave toys strewn round the garden invitingly
the garage doors are always open and the car is dirty
the garden shed is full of muddy tools and spiders
the number made of no-polish brass needs polishing
it has a satellite dish and a cable and a fake alarm-box
the locks are old-fashioned and destroy notions of justice
schoolkids stuff empty crisp packets into the hedge
the barbecue rusts and collects leaves in the garden
it is on my way when I pass on the other side of the road
the shutters are false and always open, leaving windows bare
the woodwork needs painting and is tinder dry
it is a stone's throw away and sometimes even closer

Owl show

Statistics, photographs, pellets as macabre
as graves, and feathers—soft-fringed secrets
displayed on card—prepare us for the show.

She pulls on gloves. Calm as a gardener,
she reaches into the box. Lifted into light
the barn owl makes us all forget the details

we have learned (facial mask, eyeballs fixed,
neck gimballed, lacerating beak down-pointed,
asymmetric openings of the ear-holes

curved to catch the evasions of its prey)
and leaves me, a vole in the silent scream,
waiting for the talons, unconsoled

that owls will never kill for fun. The box
is open. The owl flies in.
We gasp, reprieved.

Announcement

The Angel, bragging his preposterous wings
is smug enough. Folding his hands, he tilts
his smarmy little face, one eyebrow raised
to show she isn't *his* choice. Hunched

and robed in heavy chocolate, she needs
some urgent care. The perfect, modern loggia,
the hint of meadow, forest, paradise outside—
all of them mock her gut-kicked doubt. We know

that *she* believes, and gasping, crosses hands,
her fingers trembling like the spirit-seed
she fears is lodged within, a burr that's hooked
into her very flesh. Her hair's like icing,

face like alabaster: childish, pale,
an ornament awaiting mantelpieces.
Devotion isn't something she can take
or leave. At twelve or thirteen, no girl could.

When the Angel's done his job, he'll flit.
Then, while the memory of his perfume fades
like sweat and ozone and cold rosemary,
she must start to make the Story up.

A soft answer

The very politest man I ever met
combed the beach at San Leone—
not to gain but to cleanse and make pure.

I had seen this mob of thundering yobbos
blundering among the temples on the hill,
fresh-liquored from their coach. . . .

My Signor Educato was no municipal
lackey. Free-lancing with his battered
canvas bag and his long arms, he cleared

all the rubbish from the subtle sweep
of sand beside the gently lapping sea.
The biggest of the shaven-headed louts

began the ritual this evening, with the sun
sinking into the water like a polished shield.
He spat the formula into the old man's face

as he straightened up. 'Does any Bastard in this
town . . . ' and paused and the other thugs,
in terrace-chorus, joined, 'speak fuckin *English!*'

My paragon, he merely smiled, and in a voice
of perfect calm, in pure Italian, replied,
'No, ma per voi, gentilissimi Signori, imparerei volentieri.'

ROSS KIGHTLY